HERE I AM!
WHO ARE YOU?

HERE I AM! WHO ARE YOU?

Resolving conflicts between
adults and children

Jesper Juul

Translated by Hayes van der Meer

authorHOUSE®

AuthorHouse™
1663 Liberty Drive
Bloomington, IN 47403
www.authorhouse.com
Phone: 1-800-839-8640

www.jesperjuul.com
www.family-lab.com
www.artofsayingno.tv
www.familylab.com.au

Other English titles:

Your Competent Child, published by Balboa Press
Your Competent Child DVD at www.textalk.se

English titles published by AuthorHouse:

Family Life
Family Time
No!

Published by AuthorHouse   07/27/2012

ISBN: 978-1-4685-7933-8 (sc)
ISBN: 978-1-4685-7934-5 (hc)
ISBN: 978-1-4685-7935-2 (e)

CONTENTS

INTRODUCTION

This book is essentially about "boundaries" and what used to be called "setting limits" for children. It is all about how we define ourselves without harming anyone.

The love we feel for our children and for others means one thing to us but something different to them. They experience our love differently to the way we do and it all depends on how we are able to convert our loving feelings into loving behavior.

We all feel love differently. However, we have one thing in common: we do not feel loved when our personal boundaries are being violated or not treated with respect.

If the violations are severe or regular we lose our sense of self-worth and thereby our ability to function constructively. Then we are not able to take care of ourselves or improve on the relationships with those who offend us. This applies to adults and children alike.

It takes time to get to know our own boundaries. Some we know by instinct but others it will take us years to understand and define.

It is one of life's curious paradoxes that we only get to know where our boundaries lie when others cross them. Likewise, we are only able to find out where other people's boundaries are when we cross theirs—and perhaps even violate them.

When we interact with colleagues, friends and strangers in our daily lives a number of protocols apply so we avoid violating their boundaries more often than is necessary. These vary from one culture to the other and from one group of people to the next. Nevertheless, they all require us to keep a certain *distance* so as not to offend anyone.

Family life is exactly opposite: it is all about *closeness.*

Young children's need for *closeness* may seem never ending—although they also do need breathing space and distance. They do not instinctively know their parents boundaries and will only learn about these as they happen to cross them.

Exactly this is one of the valuable gifts children offer their parents: the opportunity to learn about their own personal boundaries and alter them so they work for everyone. This is also the case with partnerships between adults. The difference between your child and your partner is that your child has much less experience to draw on. Nevertheless, it will take about ten years for anyone to get used to another person's boundaries.

The better we understand our boundaries the more *personally* we are able to express them—and the more satisfying our relationships will be.

The love between parents and children is so strong (and vulnerable) that we constantly run the risk of crossing each others' boundaries. This is inevitably part of any family's mutual learning process. When parents are able to set the tone and take the lead the children's guilt lessens while their understanding of self grows.

Our opinions and beliefs about children and child-rearing are more or less deliberate and well-considered. More often than not they are also inconsistent. For some people their opinions and beliefs are more important than life itself. Others internalize these but they become part of their conversations with others anyway.

Some people clearly state: "I *am* what I believe in!" Nevertheless, we were *ourselves* before we formed our opinions and beliefs and without them we are also *ourselves*.

When we become parents this is exactly what we need more than anything else: *to be ourselves*.

This book is an invitation. An invitation to define yourself, your opinions and beliefs—and reflect on mine. It is not about assessing what is "right" or "wrong", or judge "guilty" or "not guilty". It is an invitation to develop your confidence wherever possible and to acknowledge doubt whenever necessary.

WHO DECIDES?

Within the confines of the family, parents make the decisions. At crèche, child care, kindergarten and at school other adults decide what happens. Although children know a lot about life they lack the necessary life experience, worldly knowledge and the developmental skills to be able to take control. There is no doubt that it is better for children that adults make the decisions.

It is however, very important *what* the adults decide and for the children's health and well-being it is even more important *how* they decide. It matters greatly whether adults do this in a rigid, dictatorial fashion or are impetuous and flexible or make decisions on the spur of the moment. It also matter if the decisions actually make sense.

Children, as well as adults, thrive better when the decisions make sense—as much sense as possible. This can only happen when parents carefully consider which *values* they want as part of their family. Some of these values we are consciously aware of, others we have never given a thought. Some values we might never define at all but we constantly express them through what we say and do.

—It is important that children obey their parents simply because they know best.

—It is important that children in a democratic society are part of making the decisions.

—It is important that children learn to believe in God.

—It is important that children learn to respect others.

—It is important that children develop self-confidence.

—It is important that children know how to look after the environment.

—It is important that children do well at school.

It is not that long ago when most of our family values were based on moral or religious beliefs. Parents knew what was right and wrong. Since then, our knowledge about children has grown enormously and today we know much more about how children function and develop. Much of what our parents and grandparents thought was right has indeed turned out not to be so.

For many very good reasons today's parents find it challenging to make decisions on behalf of their children. It is important that we as parents decide, but it is also important that these decisions equip our children with the best possible developmental opportunities. In other words; we need to let go of some of the power we used to have—without letting go of our leadership. This is, in fact, a very difficult task which very few of us master straight away. We can only work this out together with our children as they grow up.

This reciprocal process of learning will inevitably lead to conflicts and frustrations. From time to time, everyone will get angry, become sad and feel frustrated. This is the way it ought to be. Conflicts between children and parents are not an indication that the parents are not good parents or are not doing things properly. Children, as well as adults, learn so much from conflicts and in healthy families the parents take responsibility for those conflicts. If, or when, parents pass the blame onto the children many more conflicts will follow. This is also irresponsible leadership.

POWER

We mostly associate our interactions with children with love, care and responsibility. We do not often think that power is an important aspect of these relationships. Nevertheless, parents do hold the power over their children's lives and well-being. During the first couple of years, parents have complete power and as the children grow older parents still have most of the power.

Parents have legal, financial, physical and psychological power—even when they feel most powerless. In most Scandinavian countries, the fact is that the abuse of power is greatest when adults feel most powerless or when they, for various reasons, do not want to take responsibility for their power. In other cultures, the abuse of power—at times physical violence—is a virtue and often seen as the only responsible method of bringing up children.

In Scandinavia, physical violence is no longer a recognized or approved method of bringing up children. Some parents still hit and smack but most are aware that this form of violence is not only hurtful to the one who is being hit but also to the one who hits[1]. They have now become so civilized that they disassociate themselves from violence as a source of power. Likewise, they are beginning to acknowledge that there might not be any real difference between physical violence and psychological or emotional violence such as ridiculing, putting down, criticizing, sarcasm and slander. Any form of violence is degrading.

It was much easier to get children to obey and do as they were told when parents used violence—or threatened to use violence. Some people remember this as "the good old days". The adults set the limits and if the children did not obey then all hell would break loose: "If they don't want to listen—they must feel!" There was a general consensus that this was acceptable. Parents and teachers thought it was their duty to teach children the difference between right and wrong—and violence was the way to get the message across.

Using violence as a way of raising children does not create respect—instead it creates fear. It does not teach children the difference between right and wrong, it teaches them that using violence is alright if you have power. In exactly the same way, this will not teach children to respect their parents' boundaries, it will teach them to fear the consequences if they cross them[2].

---

[1]   Jesper Juul, Dit kompetente barn, Kbh. 1995, s. 110 ff.

[2]   Jesper Juul, Dit kompetente barn, Kbh. 1995, s. 173 ff.

When violence is being phased out it leaves a kind of void in the relationship between adults and children. Parents are now experimenting with different ways of filling this void. Some try the idea of democracy but tire of the endless discussions. Others try to be guided by the children's likes and dislikes but end up getting lost. Some hand over responsibility to the children but end up with many very draining power struggles. Yet others are so focused on creating space for the children and pay them so much attention that there is no room left for themselves and their personal needs.

All of these experiments have been necessary for us to work out how we can use our adult power more constructively than previous generations have been able to. Neither children nor adults are harmed by these experiments—not even when they fail. It is not until we are locked in, stubborn and unable to change direction that both adults and children are unable to thrive.

For centuries, all you had to do was become a father or a mother and you would automatically assume authority. This made it reasonably easy for parents to exercise their power. It is not like that anymore—at least not after the first couple of years of infancy. Today's parents have to develop an authority which is far more *personal* if they are going to assume leadership and avoid abusing their power.

Parents and teachers are no longer able to automatically demand respect simply because of *what* they are. It is more about *who* they are. Children (and adults) have lost respect for those in power. Slowly but surely personal credibility is a deciding factor in how much respect and how much personal and pedagogical power we have.

POWER AND RESPONSIBILITY

In this book we will focus on parents' and educators' psychological/emotional power. We do this for two reasons: it plays a significant role in our daily interactions with children. Of the various types of power parents and educators have over children this is also the least tangible and most difficult one to define.

Our genes determine our children's gender, physique, some disabilities, their looks and perhaps even their temperament. Their personality, the way they see themselves and even their ability to use their intellect and live and work with others depends on how others *relate* to them. As parents we obviously have the greatest influence on this. Grandparents, teachers and others with whom they connect also play a significant role.

In my profession as a family therapist we consider the process of living together as the most important factor for the well-being of the family.

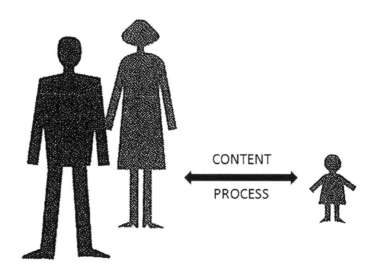

Content—Process

Content refers to what we do, what we talk about and the boundaries and traditions we have within the family.

Process refers to the way we do things. The way we communicate, the mood and atmosphere of the way we interact with one another.

Professionals no longer refer to speaking "nicely" or "sensibly" as opposed to "rudely" or "unintelligently". Instead we refer to ways of doing things as being constructive or healthy for the family whereas others are destructive and unhealthy.

When the interactions within the family are destructive it is inevitably destructive for all members. Some might notice this before others and indeed feel it more profoundly but everyone will suffer. The same applies when the interaction are constructive. Everyone thrives and benefits.

When it comes to the relations between adults and children, the adults are always and single handedly responsible for the quality of the interaction. Children are simply not *able* to take that responsibility. Nevertheless, at times they are forced to because the adults are *unable* to. The end result is always destructive for everyone involved.

This has caused much confusion and frustration for parents and others who since the mid 1970s have attempted to democratically share power with children. Without much further questioning the adults thought that the children were able to share responsibility when they were sharing the power.

However, it does not work like that. Children are able to be part of deciding what is for dinner but they are not able to take responsibility for the atmosphere around the dining table. Children can be part of deciding where to spend Christmas but they cannot take responsibility for how the family interacts during the holiday break. Even young students are able to decide which topics they would like to work on but they cannot and should not share any of the responsibility for the atmosphere in the classroom.

Responsibility for the quality of the interactions cannot be handed over to the children—or even shared with them. This responsibility must always lie with the adults. It is in fact the most important responsibility parents have. It is also in this manner they exercise their most subtle and indirect power.

Traditionally, parents have accepted responsibility when everything went well and there was a constructive atmosphere in the family but pushed some of it away when the opposite happened. It is still like that in most families. When the interaction between children and adults fail then parents (and teachers) blame the children. This is not only irresponsible it is also unethical because it destroys their appetite and enthusiasm for life.

The alternative is *not* that parents start blaming themselves. This does not do anyone any good. The only constructive alternative is for the parents to take responsibility for what has happened and try to make sure it does not happen again.

For generations we have believed that the emotions we incorrectly label as "negative" (anger, fury, irritation, etc.) were harmful. It is not that simple. Our attempt to do what we think is "right" is often just as destructive.

An example:

A young couple were worried about a number of things regarding their 18 month old daughter: "Every now and then she will sit right in front of the freezer, point at it and say: "Want ice cream!" The first couple of times we thought is was rather cute and quite clever. However, it can take us up to 30 minutes to get her to stop. We experience a similar pattern in other situations when she doesn't want to do what we want her to do. How can we deal with that?"

It is a very common reaction from parents of this generation. They are thoughtful and well-informed. They are up-to-date with the latest parenting trends and know what is being said and written about raising children, and they are very open and willing to talk honestly about their opinions and experiences. They do not believe in authoritarian parenting and make sure their daughter gets all the attention she needs when she is with them.

They are not angry or irritated with the daughter but they are aware that the developments could be unfortunate—and they are right.

The following happens (**content**): The daughter announces that she wants an ice cream. Her father considers the request and decides that he does not want to give her one right now. He says: "No Caroline, you can't have an ice cream now!" Caroline says: "Want one!" so he says: "No Caroline, you can't have an ice cream now. We're going to have dinner soon!"

Caroline gets frustrated, slams her hand on the floor and repeats what she wants. So he repeats what he said and adds: " . . . If you have an ice cream now then you won't be able to eat dinner." Caroline get more frustrated and so the exchange continues until Caroline starts crying. Then her father picks her up and carries her out of the kitchen.

The father's motives are important. He does not want to be authoritarian and therefore tries hard to make Caroline understand why he has decided that she cannot have any ice cream. Ideally he would like to reach some kind of consensus and hopes that Caroline will understand his reasoning and agree with him. He did not scold instead he spoke in earnest and kept eye contact with her. Both parents use a similar approach when

Caroline does not want to go to bed, come home from child care, when she wants to wear inappropriate clothing, etc.

They try to avoid emotional conflicts with Caroline. During their own upbringings they had many uncomfortable experiences with such conflicts. Both of them attended kindergartens where the staff tried to convince them that any conflict can be dealt with by using reasoning, logic and common sense. They also learned that it is wrong to be "unreasonable". The conflict with Caroline makes them feel like they are bad parents.

The following happens (**process**): The father tries to seek consensus and stays at the same level as Caroline for a long time. He experiences her increased frustration as an indication that he is not succeeding as a parent. As a consequence the leadership (responsibility for the situation) is passed on to Caroline. She notices through his voice, facial expression and body language that he feels uncomfortable and she is put in a position where she assumes responsibility for whether or not he looks happy or sad. In other words, she ends up with the responsibility for her father's well-being and for how long the conflict lasts. No child is able to shoulder such responsibility. When they try anyway it looks like they want to take over the family—dominate, decide and be in charge.

Children are not interested in power. When they begin to tyrannize it is because the parents are not taking leadership. Their behavior is not "unreasonable" because they are power-hungry. It is an expression of the pain they feel because they have been given far too much responsibility.

Caroline's parents are in a difficult situation. They only know one alternative, namely their own parents' solution:

"Don't make a fuss! If you don't listen and do as you are told, you go straight to bed!" or "Please do the right thing. I will get very angry if you don't stop being naughty!"

However, they better not repeat their parents critical degrading, authoritarian and deeply insulting way of defining their boundaries.

So what is Caroline's father to do next time she sits in front of the freezer, slams the floor and demands ice cream?

He could do this: First time she says: "Want ice cream!" he could say: "No Caroline, you can't have an ice cream now! We are going to have dinner soon." The second time: "Caroline, I am not going to give you an ice cream now!" and look her kindly in the eyes. If she insists on the ice cream, he looks away, moves away and starts doing something else.

If Caroline is an otherwise healthy child she might try a few more times and then she will begin to cry. (I shall deal with this reaction a bit later in this book.)

Most parents will inevitably be confronted by this suggestion and wonder:

—But, doesn't she feel rejected?
—Yes, hopefully she will! That is exactly the point.

What parents need to do is very simple, yet it is not necessarily all that easy. It only works if they *mean* what they say and do it with a *clear conscience*. In this case only those two elements create the *"personal authority"* which is fundamental if no one is to be degraded and feel they are wrong.

19

None of what happened is wrong. There is nothing wrong in asking for an ice cream when you would like one. Neither is there anything wrong in deciding that it is not the right time for an ice cream. Nevertheless, the situation escalated in a way where both Caroline and her parents felt that they were wrong. The parents were far from irresponsible. They just did not know how to use their power to take constructive responsibility.

BOUNDARIES

Broadly speaking, there are two types of boundaries: *General* boundaries and *Personal* boundaries. Parents will get to know both types during the 15 to 20 years (or more) they live with their children. The first six to seven years they will be confronted by new ones almost daily. Then there is a break and when the children turn 12 or 13 it all starts again.

Some of our own personal boundaries existed well before we had children. Wisely, we let go of some of them the very first time the little baby looks us in the eyes. Others we hang on to and others still we modify as we get to know our children—and get a better understanding of who we are.

Knowing our boundaries and being able to express them is not a requirement for entering into parenthood. It is indeed a life-long process of learning which develops in conjunction with our parents, our partners, our children, their partners and the grandchildren.

General boundaries

General boundaries are those generally accepted in certain environments. This is the way to do things—and not do them—in this society, family, school, club, etc. These are the commonly accepted norms in the particular culture we belong to or visit.

The general boundaries which we would like to apply in our own home ought to be thought through and considered carefully. We also need to make sure we are willing to fully integrate them.

Up until the early sixties there was a broad consensus about the general boundaries. They were expressed and upheld in a similar manner throughout society. Everything was reasonably predictable. Things have changed. Parents and other adults can no longer simply justify the general boundaries by saying: "That's just not the way things are done!" Today's children only need to turn on the television or speak with their friends to work out that everyone does things differently and there is not "one way of doing things". More and more adults are also reluctant to accept conformity—and this is a very positive development.

The things we often refer to as "norms" are part of the general boundaries. Some parents say: "It is important for the children's safety and well-being that they understand the norms and boundaries." Others ask more cautiously: "Is it really that important that our children fit into the norms and have boundaries?"

The term "norms" encompasses the routines of the family, their traditions, tasks and duties. Some families are very set in their ways of doing things perhaps out of necessity because the parents are busy working. Others are set in their ways due to religious convictions, and still others due to their belief in certain pedagogical principles.

Some families follow a set of norms simply because the parents feel insecure when they are presented with too many choices while others follow fixed norms predetermined by the authoritarian society they live in. Others still would prefer to live with set norms as supposed to unemployment and social welfare.

Personally, I find it difficult to understand the purpose of set and fixed "norms". It is my experience that parents who most forcefully uphold these are the ones who find it difficult to control their children—with or without strict limits and boundaries.

Those parents actually have a lot in common with most other parents and teachers. When we attempt to change children's behavior but do not succeed we often resort to doing more of the same—just for a longer period of time. This reaction is as common as it is unwise. Upon consideration it does not make sense but we do it anyway—all of us.

The fact is that most children and parents thrive with certain norms and boundaries. We need to get up in the morning and go to bed at night. We need to work, develop interests and take pride in some of our family traditions.

However, I do not know if any norms are better than others. In the first instance the adults define the norms and boundaries of the family and if they are able to modify these as the family grows and develops then there are no limits for what the children can live with. This is not harmful in any way.

The current, and at times passionate, debate about the need for children to have boundaries lacks one important dimension: we forget the extend to which the daily routines of children has changed during the past 30 years.

We have softened the psychological and existential strictness which children were exposed to both at school and at home. The focus is changing. Today there is a lesser focus on *control* and *obedience* and a greater focus on *responsibility* and *personal growth*. In the meantime however, society has developed in a manner which forces children to comply with some strict structures.

These days it would benefit many children and their parents if they were able to spend more time together—especially the first two or three years of the children's lives. They are being looked after by a range of different people who often forget to prepare the children for what is happening in their lives—the carers' lives that is. When they are going on holidays, look for a new job and have other changes in their lives. There can be a real sense of "now you see me, now you don't!" The routines of the institutions and the working conditions of the staff often makes it difficult for them to greet the children and farewell them properly without it being a forced "What do you say when you leave . . . ?" It is furthermore often impossible for them to stay with one carer during prolonged periods of time.

Children are forced to adapt to a number of different family situations as their parents divorce, move, meet new partners and introduce bonus families with different children and other relatives. There are people the children are forced to spend time with and some they are not able to see. Sometimes the parents share the children and they have to relate to two different homes, struggle with the challenges of packing school bags and sports gear in advance. Add to this the expectation that they participate in the daily family activities either because it is a practical necessity or because their parents want to prepare them for "real" life.

Very few adults would be able to cope with such a lifestyle without becoming seriously frustrated and stressed.

Neither can the children. It is very unfortunate that many of them are diagnosed and forced into some kind of treatment—often medical. Yet, adults in similar situations are encouraged to take time off, go on sick leave and "look after themselves". In my opinion this way of treating our children is both unprofessional and unethical. I find it hard to understand how parents and experts can accept to take part in any of this.

Many children are living over-structured lives but it is not possible to compensate for this by lifting the boundaries within the family. When we as parents are frustrated and feel we are about to lose control we resort to putting in place structures to help us cope. For the sake of the children we really ought to consider whether *more* boundaries and limits are the answer.

Most children find it easy to conform and live with general boundaries. They do this all the time, at child care, at school, at their sports club, with their friends, etc. There is only one condition: that their personal boundaries are not violated—or indeed completely ignored and disregarded.

25

Personal boundaries

The word *personal* means that these boundaries are individual and unique. They are there because parents have different personalities and tempers, they have different backgrounds, values, moods and so forth.

—I don't want you to play music right now. I have a head ache.

—No, I don't want to read you a story right now. I prefer to read the newspaper.

—I don't want you to hit me. Please tell me what makes you angry.

—I would like to help you write that paper but it has to be today or tomorrow. The rest of the week I am busy.

—I don't want you to sleep in our bed anymore. I want your mother and I to sleep on our own.

—No, I don't want to bake a pizza today. I prefer to make meat balls instead.

—I understand that you would like to stay at home from school today but I don't want to take the day off work.

—Yes, I do want to play with you—in 30 minutes when I have finished doing the dishes.

—I understand that it is important for you to go to that party. Right now I cannot give you an answer, I don't know if I want you to go. Let me think about it till tomorrow. I need that time to work out what I think. . . . no, I am not going to give you an answer right now!

—Yes, the dress you wore at Grandma's birthday is very pretty and you look beautiful in it but I don't want you to wear it at child care. It is not warm enough. . . . no, because it is cold outside and because I don't want you to wear it!

Later in this book I shall get back to some of those boundaries. Let us first take a look at what characterizes them.

They use a *personal* language: "I want . . ." and "I don't want . . ." They clearly state: *Here I am! This is the way I am and this is what I believe in!* The child is not in doubt about what the father or mother thinks, feels or wants. There is a personal contact and the *personal* language is always *warm* no matter if the answer is "Yes!" or "No!" Any expression which is not *personal* makes a positive connection impossible and this influences the outcome.

People often claim that "children test the limits". They say this as if the children consciously do it to see how far they can go and if they can manipulate their parents. In my experience this is not the case at all.

The children they talk about are those children who do not feel certain about the contact with their parents—who in turn are insecure about their contact with the children. Those parents hardly ever use *personal* language thus the children are not able to work out what their parents stand for. Sure, the children try to find their parents' boundaries and limits but they do this simply because they cannot work out where they are. When you do not know where your parents' boundaries are you become confused, insecure, either completely passive or hyperactive—and definitely *lonely.*

Children do not want to *look* for the boundaries neither do they want to *test* them. What they do is *lack* contact. They might not necessarily need more physical presence but they need a connection. It is not a question about communicating more but a question of the quality of what is being said.

The children feel lonely not because their parents do not love them. The problem is that parents often find it difficult to express their love. The same is also true for adult relationships. If your partner never expresses what he/she wants or does not want and what she/he thinks and feels, you will become lonely in the relationship. No matter how loving and considerate your partner might otherwise be.

Children's language is already *personal*. When they ask for something they always want two things: an ice cream/a story/a new bike *and* contact. They can get by without the ice cream and all the other things but not without the contact. The children are not consciously aware of this themselves, they think the ice cream is what it is all about. Some parents are led to believe that too. It is important to understand that the *contact* is more important.

Our language does not become personal simply because we replace "you" with "I". It needs to be said in earnest. We need to speak from the heart. Sometimes it is perfectly clear what we stand for, other times we can slowly feel the revelation: "I see . . . that is how I feel about it!"

When we speak from the heart the emphasis will automatically be right. You will no longer say: "This is my *opinion!*" but: "This is *my* opinion!" For most of us this requires personal reflection and a lot of practice. We must experiment (and accept defeat) and preferably do it with the children. It is obviously beneficial if we are able to reflect and talk to other adults as well.

Let us return to the topic of *boundaries.* Apart from being personal they must also be worthy and fair. The adult's point of view must be communicated without ulterior motives and conditions. They must not be critical or down grade the children.

It is easy to cooperate when it can be done on the basis of worthiness and fairness—for children and adults alike. If we have to try to cooperate with anything else we are forced to give in, put up with other people's conditions or put up a fight.

It is good for the children to get a clear understanding of why their mother's and father's boundaries are exactly where they are. This explanation will need to be brief, clear, truthful and without manipulation or convincing motives.

We will not be able to logically explain all our personal boundaries—not even to ourselves. This obviously makes it even more difficult for children to understand them. Fortunately, it does not make the boundaries more difficult to respect. Children do not respect their parents' boundaries simply because they can be justified. Children respect the boundaries because they respect the *person.* Stories made up on the spot to cover for a particular situation will only weaken the boundaries. It is better to tell the truth: "I am not sure why I think like that, but I do, and this is the way I want it!"

This is exceptional role modeling. The children will benefit from being able to do the same when they need to decide whether or not to take drugs, alcohol, get involved with criminal behavior, and the like. "I am not sure why I don't want that, but I don't!" It is of invaluable comfort for them to know that it is alright to listen to their inner voice even when the peer pressure is heavy and they are not able to explain or reason for their point of view.

My boundaries?

A number of our boundaries date back to our own childhoods. This is obviously a mixed bag. Some of the boundaries have been passed on through generations and go as far back as our parents' childhoods. A great deal of these make sense and were handed to us with love and respect. If they work it makes sense to pass them on to future generations.

Other boundaries made sense 25 years ago but are no longer relevant. General developments in society make it necessary to introduce boundaries our parents could not have anticipated.

Our parents also set boundaries which were unreasonable and enforced these in hurtful and degrading ways. Sometimes violating our personal boundaries. We consciously distance ourselves from these and promise that we will never treat our own children like that—but we end up doing it anyway!

This is not because we are stupid or forgetful. We do it because we love our parents and trusted them. We cooperated [1] with them and when we were hurt we concluded that we were

---

[1]   Jesper Juul, Dit kompetente barn, Kbh. 1995, s. 39 ff.

at fault, we were to blame and deserved the treatment we received. We genuinely thought it was our own fault.

Most of us have completely forgotten what hurt us the most. The pain was so intense that we repressed it. When we have our own children these feelings will without doubt resurface. Not necessarily as pain but as a repetition of our parents' actions. If we are not careful there is a serious risk that we pass this pain on without taking responsibility for it.

Fortunately, most of us choose to have children with partners whose painful experiences are completely different to ours. This makes it easier to notice their pain than it is to recognize our own. It is a good idea for us to pay careful attention to when we become frustrated with our children. The irritation and frustration is sometimes irrational and does not make sense. This is often because we touch some very sore point—in spite of our promises not to repeat the past.

This is what we inherit. Add to it a substantial amount of junk which we collect. Stuff from the television, various teachers, brothers and sisters, friends and neighbors, and from books and lectures. Some of it fits perfectly while other parts do not fit *our* family at all.

To find out if this is useful we just have to listen to: "The parents' automatic telephone answering machine" as I call it. It is the one which automatically starts playing when children are within earshot. It most certainly plays when we take the children shopping, visit friends, dine out, etc.

It is the one which says: "Remember to wipe your shoes!" while the children are busy taking them off. It says: "Remember to say "Hello!" and shake hands!" when they are just about to do it of their own accord. Within four to five years children learn to turn a deaf ear to the actual words but they do hear the real message: "You would never be able to get anything right if I wasn't here to remind you!"

It is a worthwhile exercise for parents to listen to what they are really saying. If we are honest about it we do not actually believe in half of what we automatically say. The rest can do with some serious editing without much getting lost.

The important question is whether or not there are boundaries which are beneficial and necessary *for* children. Of course we must stop them when they are about to cross a busy road—but these precautions are obvious.

Parents need to ask themselves this: "Which boundaries do I personally need in order for me to feel comfortable about myself and my children?" and "How do I define myself in relation to the children for us to be able to nourish the closeness and contact we all desire?"

Today's parents have experienced something previous generations have not. They have spent more time with professionals (child carers, teachers) than they have with their own parents. They have seen and experienced how these professionals handle different situations but they often do not know how their parents would. They are lacking this know-how.

Professionals have to be *professional.* Amongst other things this means: *not*-personal. They aim to act in accordance with various educational theories and certain regulations. They are by no means cold or disengaged but it is all about "head" instead of "heart". This is often a good thing as we tend to act inappropriately when we follow our emotions and react spontaneously. However, it is not a good way of being a parent.

It is a great idea to let yourself be inspired by teachers, books, television shows, and so forth. On the other hand it is not a good idea to try to parent by following various theories and ideals instead of following your own beliefs. It is harmful and detrimental to the vital personal contact between parents and children. Things go completely wrong when parents follow a predetermined ideology which they themselves and their children have to fit in with. It really does not matter whether this ideology is religious, political, pedagogical or philosophical.

It is much better for us and our children when we aim to be ourselves rather than try to "do the right thing". Parents who are authentic are better parents than those who try to be theoretical parents. Parents who make mistakes and take responsibility for their mistakes are better parents than those who try to be perfect. Parents who strive for perfection will always make their children feel like failures and children who feel like failures often end up failing.

Two parents—two sets of boundaries

It used to be said that: "Parents should not contradict each other when raising their children!" This was a mantra of the times when parents were also warned that the children would seize power if they were given a chance to do so. In many ways parenting was considered a power struggle between adults and children. A battle which the adults obviously had to win. This meant that they had to present a united front against the children.

Today's parents have a number of options. One is to consider the relationship with your children as a power struggle. Then a united front is important. I would not recommend this but it is indeed an option.

Another option is to strive for *equality*. [2] Equality between man and woman, and between adults and children provides the best opportunity for everyone to develop healthy relationships. It also fosters closeness and a sense of community.

When relationships are equal it is possible to see each other's differences and acknowledge that these are an important part of strengthening the community. However, it is not easy to make this happen—especially not for parents who themselves grew up in families and societies where conformity was seen as the ideal and diversity a threat.

Each parent brings to the family different experiences, different personalities, different values and different genders (mostly). Even though parents are able to reach an intellectual agreement about their parenting style and which boundaries are important their individual ways of implementing these will always vary. This applies to the *general* boundaries in particular. Their *personal* boundaries have always been and will always be different.

Every now and then the differences between two parents will cause problems. This is unavoidable and when it happens

---

[2]   Jesper Juul, Dit kompetente barn, Kbh. 1995, s. 16 ff og s. 35 ff.

you can choose to see it as a *problem* which has to be dealt with *before* you can take the next steps, or as a *challenge* which can help the family take the *next* steps. At first most of us will see this as a problem and it takes a little while before we see the opportunities.

The challenges are always the same: Parents need to examine their own and each other's points of view. "Why do I feel the way I do?" and "What makes you feel the way you do?" It might be challenging and even confronting to dig into our experiences, as we will inevitably uncover something about ourselves which is less then flattering.

The most important shared point of reference must be that no one per definition is *right*. This is important for two reasons: Firstly, because parents each possess roughly half of what it takes to make a family happen. The other half they must develop together. One parent does not know it all and cannot do it all on their own. Our aims must not be to create a family that is "right" but one that is *ours*. If we end up with power struggles in the family there are no winners—only losers.

Families with two parents will always have a mixture of masculine and feminine values. Fathers can *also* represent feminine values just like mothers *also* can represent the masculine. Some parents are able to do this due to their upbringing others learn it as they grow. Either way, the values will at times be of opposing nature and cause conflicts, at other times they melt together very smoothly.

An example:

A couple came to see me and the father shared this story: "We have two daughters, one is four and a half years old, the other is seven months. My wife and I have a harmonious life—even after the eldest was born—and we looked forward to number two. Linda (the eldest) was excited about the prospect of a younger sister and she would often sit with her hands on my wife's pregnant belly and tell her sister all sorts of things.

When Susan arrived Linda was initially very fond of her. She would pat her, help change her and was proud to show her off to anyone and everyone. Everything was harmonious and total bliss—until a few months ago.

When I sit down with both of them on my lap everything is just fine until the youngest gets a fright and starts crying. It took me a little while to work out what was happening but Linda would slide her arm under mine and pull Susan's hair really hard, pinch her or something similar.

I know that Linda might be jealous of Susan and this is not the issue I want to ask you about. I would like to know if I am handling the situation the wrong way. When Susan's hair has been pulled, she has been pinched or whatever I put the little one on the couch and try to calm her. Then I pick up the eldest, carry her into her bedroom and put her on the bed. I tell her off and tell her to be nice to her sister. Is this wrong? If so, what should I do instead?"

My answer to these parents was: "Yes, I do think it is wrong! I would like to suggest a different course of action. Before I do that I need to explain to you how I interpret what Linda does.

This will enable you to decide whether or not you think it is worthwhile trying what I suggest.

"Sibling jealousy" is a somewhat old-fashioned description of what happens inside Linda. She is not jealous in the same way adults are jealous. She is in the process of adjusting to the changes within your family. In her experience this is a huge change and challenge. For you to understand what it is like you need to try to imagine what it would be like for you if your wife came home one day and told you that she wanted to live with two men. Then she tells you that her second husband will move in next week. This would be such a profound shakeup of your lifestyle that it would take time to get used to—even without the feelings of jealousy.

There is only half as much time, half as much room and half as much attention as there used to be. This is a loss of monumental proportions no matter if you are four or forty years old. It is possible that she might become jealous but this does not happen in six months unless parents constantly and seriously treat them differently. Adult siblings can be jealous with each other so we assume that this also applies to much younger siblings. This is rarely the case.

That was one of the reasons for Linda pulling Susan's hair. The other reason is that she is in fact *cooperating*. All children cooperate. They either imitate or copy their parents. Sometimes they do this directly and sometime by doing the opposite. In your case Linda copies you directly. Her little sister was a dream come true for you. Both you and your wife agreed to have her, you were excited and fell in love with her straight away. So was Linda. She arrived during a harmonious period of your lives. Linda was part of that. The family was full of love, care and happiness. So was Linda.

The difference between you and Linda is that for her it was in fact quite *difficult* to get a little sister. Her feelings are not exclusively positive and happy, they are also sad and frustrated. She has felt like that for six months and kept a close eye on you to see if you would also feel like that. She needed to know how you would deal with such feelings—but that is not how you felt. As a result Linda has come to the conclusion that her feelings were wrong. She tried to repress these feelings but at some stage she was no longer able to do that.

Pulling Susan's hair is in fact a clever way for a four-year-old to deal with this. She is not able to walk up to her parents and say: "Listen folks, the two of you constantly seem so happy with the little one. I like her too but it is not so easy for me to get used to the risk that I might have to be on my own for a little while a number of times during the day while you do things with her. I am beginning to feel guilty that I am not able to think everything is total bliss. What am I supposed to do?"

When I answer your question in a rather straight forward manner it is simply because I do not think children should be punished for cooperating.

Allow me to suggest the following: Next time it happens you make sure the little one calms down. Then you put Linda on you lap, hold her close and give her a kiss. You say something along the lines of: "Linda, I suddenly realize that you must be irritated with your sister every now and then. I haven't thought of this until you pulled her hair. Perhaps this is because I haven't been irritated with her—yet! Do you think she takes up too much space in our family?"

Use your own words so it comes from your heart. There is no need to criticize what she did. She does not need to know that *it* was wrong. She already knows that. She needs to know that is not *her* who is wrong. The best way you can make sure she understands that is by acknowledging her feelings."

Both parents became visibly touched. The father because he knew his usual actions did not work and he was pleased to have an alternative. The mother started crying for a completely different reason. She explained: "I knew that what my husband did was wrong but I told myself that it was because he was too tough. I would have been softer. Perhaps I often do that: criticize him for being tough instead of trying to work out what is really going on."

The mother's final comment reveals a conflict between the masculine and the feminine. Something most parents will be challenged by. Sometimes fathers *are* too square and sometimes mothers *are* too round but that really is not important. What matters is that they are *relevant* when they define their boundaries. An indication that they might be following the wrong path is when an inner unease and doubt appears. That is exactly what made this father step up and ask the question. When you feel unease and doubt it is time to stop and think before you continue the old pattern.

It is important to make sense and agree on what to do in a situation such as the above as it relates to *general* boundaries ("In this family we do not want people attacking each other physically.") Nevertheless, there will always be differences when it comes to the parents' *personal* boundaries.

When these differences become an issue it is important to remember that two people are involved: one parent and one child. It is not enough to consider what is "best for the child". It is just as important to discuss what is good for the parent who is involved.

"What is it you would like to achieve?" is the first and very important question. When that has been answered the next question should be: "How can you achieve that without violating the child's integrity?" If that is not possible then you will need to ask: "Is it actually reasonable to expect that of a child at this age?"

Children and boundaries

It is important for parents to remember that they must look after their own boundaries. This is not the responsibility of the child. It is equally important that the child learns to look after his or her own boundaries. This is also the parents' responsibility.

The reason why parents have this dual responsibility is that neither babies or small children are capable of looking after their boundaries. They are capable of making others aware of them but they cannot protect themselves against violations or abuse.

When a child experiences that their boundaries matter to adults, they will in turn learn to care for others' boundaries. When a child's boundaries are violated by adults, they will in turn either become aggressive and violate those of others or become introverted and self-destructive. In the western world it is most often the boys who react aggressively and the girls who react in a self-destructive manner—although this is changing.

Very often children will try to violate the boundaries of those who violate theirs. This is not in an attempt to take out revenge. When this happens within a family they do it because violations are part of that family's culture and they experience it as their parents' way of expressing love. They have complete faith in their parents' judgement.

Much of what we have come to know as good and loving upbringing is in fact offensive to the children. Many parents have been able to sense this but have remained silent out fear of being seen as irresponsible. This is unfortunate at a time when the children need their parents' genuine love the most.

This sentiment is hovering just below the surface and it ends up influencing their actions especially when they become frustrated or uncertain. There is in fact a easy solution to this: keep an eye on the child's reactions and take these seriously [3].

Infants are a good example. If you get close to an infant's face, smile and say: "Hello!" or "You certainly need to be changed! Let me do that and then I can sing you a little song and we can enjoy our time together." The baby's face will remain expressionless for five to ten seconds before it livens up and answers your approach. This is the baby's way of defining the boundary: "I need a little time to adjust before I am ready to be with you. Just be patient and I'll answer you!"

---

[3]   Jesper Juul, Dit kompetente barn, Kbh. 1995, s. 110 ff.

If the mother fails to respect this and rushes things she will cross the baby's boundaries. The baby will be stressed and instead of the smile the mother had hoped for she might get a sour face. If she then, in the hope of luring a smile, becomes really eager and begins to speak faster and louder the baby will start to cry and "cycle" with both arms and legs.

The mother now needs to make a choice—a choice every parent must make every day: "Am I going to love my child or do I need reassurance that he or she loves me?" When we become parents not all of us are mature enough to make the right choice. Children can cope with that for a while as long as they sense that you are prepared to learn. If you are not prepared to learn that, they will not love you any less—but they will love themselves less.

Children's personal boundaries are as different as adults'. Just like adults, children need time to get to know each others' boundaries. Often this does not happen until one crosses the others' boundaries.

While this learning is in progress the parents can start practicing how to respect the most obvious signals. When he spits out the vegetable puree after gulping 10 spoons it means: "No more please, I've had enough!" Look him kindly in the eyes and say: "I see, you don't want anymore now!" When she turns her head away and rejects your kiss you say: "What a pity, I would have liked a kiss but I'll just wait till next time." When he is bright awake and giggling 10 seconds after he has been put to bed you could say: "I can see that you feel more like playing—but I don't!" What we are talking about here is acknowledging and respecting children's boundaries not about self-effacing reverence.

I promised to get back to the issue of adults' boundaries and some of the ways you can clarify these. Let us also look at why this sometimes fails.

> —I don't want you to play music right now. I am really tired.

Traditionally parents would have said something along the lines of:

> —Why do you always have to play music when you *know* that I am tired?

This is a criticism in disguise. The message the child hears is: "If you loved me you would know my needs!" This is ruthless and the child will feel wronged—exactly like any adult would—be it a partner, family or friend.

> —How often do I need to tell you that I need peace and quiet when I am tired? Why is it so hard to get that in my own home?

The message is clear: "You are stupid, forgetful and treat your own father appallingly!" The father's comment is once again a criticism in disguise and the child is thereby made responsible for the father's well-being. Personal expressions tell others who we are and where our boundaries are.

Comments of this kind only tell others how unhappy we are with them.

—No, I don't want to read you a story right now. I prefer to read the newspaper.

Many parents find it difficult to prioritize their own needs. Feeling guilty about our own needs will often be expressed as a criticism of the child. All this while the child expresses his or her needs very clearly and with a clear conscience.

—Can't you see that I am reading the newspaper right now?
—Stop, you will have to wait! It is not all about you!

The child hears this message: "It is (=you are) wrong to express you desires and needs. First you ought to think about what others want." After a while of being expose to these messages the child will start expressing his or her needs indirectly by whining, pestering, manipulating, flirting, etc. Or even worse, he or she will give up completely.

It is common for parents to assert their own boundaries by violating those of the children. The message is: "You have to respect my boundaries but it is alright for me to violate yours." When parents words and actions do not connect it will always be the actions which make the biggest impression. When children are abused they are taught how to abuse. If violence is used to stop them from being violent they will most likely wait abusing others until they become adults.

—I don't want you to sleep in our bed in the future. I want your mother and I to sleep on our own.

Years ago a statement like this might have sounded like:

—You stay in you own bed otherwise you'll get a smack!
Years later it became:
—Listen darling, your mother and I have spoken about this and we think that you will soon be so big that it might be better if you no longer sleep in our bed at night. You also have your own beautiful room. Should we try and see if you can sleep there tonight? Of course you are welcome to come into us if you have a nightmare or get scared.

This is a very sweet way of thinking. It might work if you are so lucky that you say it on the exact same day she considered moving into her own bed anyway. That would be very coincidental indeed.

Even though this is a very thoughtful approach it normally does not work because it passes the responsibility to the child and leaves the decision with her.

It is perfectly alright leaving the decision with the child but only if you are also prepared to allow her making up her own mind. If that is your approach you should say: "Listen darling, your mother and I would like to sleep on our own in our bed at night. Therefore, we would like you to move into your own bed. But the decision is yours."

It is much better for the child that someone else solves a conflict like this rather than letting her be responsible for solving it. This might be challenging for modern, democratically oriented parents to accept. Nevertheless, children are not able to handle this kind of responsibility. This is evident by the way they become unreasonable and irritated.

There are three issues which are often mixed in with the discussions about children's boundaries: Their *personal* boundaries, their *needs* and their *rights*.

A number of children's general needs are being recognized as rights. This also applies to some of their personal boundaries. In many countries—certainly most European countries—governments have since the 1960 stepped in and become a safety net for the children. Seen in an historical perspective this is uncharted territory for societies and they have yet to fill this role successfully. Legislation and psychology seem to struggle when they have to work together.

Unfortunately, it is still necessary to point out the fact that children's boundaries also regard their bodies and sexuality. Most of us know that physical violence and sexual abuse are not only forbidden by law but are some of the most devastating and destructive experiences a human being can be subjected to.

Nevertheless, it happens more often than we would like to acknowledge. Adults from all levels of society abuse and violate children. These vary from country to country and from culture to culture but they are a stark reminder of how primitive our relationships with children really can be just below the surface of our otherwise civilized cultures.

We have only very recently started contemplating whether we should consider children as human beings of equal worth or whether we should hold on to the historical view that they are the *property* of the parents or the state.

Scolding?

Whether or not it is alright to scold depends on what we mean by scolding. Up until recently children have probably been *shamed* more than they have been *scolded*. Here is the difference:

Scolding: Peter, for heaven's sake, I don't want you to play with my computer when I am not here. I have said this so often and I get furious when you do it anyway! I never want that to happen again! So get away from that computer. It's mine and I don't want you on it!

Peter was *scolded* by his father. He raised his voice, yelled and had fire in his eyes. No matter if Peter is three or thirteen years old he will get a fright and perhaps even start crying. The next couple of hours their relationship will without doubt be somewhat distant and noticeably silent. This will not harm neither Peter nor their relationship. Peter crossed one of his father's boundaries once too often and received his father's spontaneous reaction smack bang in the face. That is perfectly alright—it is the way it should be.

Children often need to absorb these kind of confrontations in silence and on their own. In case Peter's silence lasts for more than a few hours his father could go to him (if he himself has calmed down, that is) and say: "I am sorry that you got a fright earlier on when I got angry with you. I did get very angry but that has passed now." Not a word about making Peter promise never to play with the computer again. No threats about what will happen if he does it anyway. This would remove Peter from the experience he has just had and hence lessen its impact.

In case Peter's mother wants to get involved or comfort him all she should do is give Peter a hug and say: "You got a fright then, huh! It isn't very nice when people yell like that." This is enough for Peter to understand that everything—except for the issue with the computer—is perfectly alright.

If she does not like her husband's reaction she will have to wait talking about this until after he and Peter have reconnected and restored their close relationship. Until then he is too vulnerable and they will most likely end up having a destructive argument.

During the brief period of time while Peter's father has lost contact with his son he might be able to speak with someone else about it—but not Peter's mother.

Shaming: Enough is enough! What were you thinking? You're a little brat! How often have I told you to keep you little fingers off my computer? Are you deaf or just stupid? Get away from that computer right now! If something has happened to it I would not like to be in your shoes . . . !"

Peter was *shamed* by his father. This criticism and degrading violates his entire existence. After a little while the father might say to Peter: "Let's be friends again!?" and Peter will be full of shame and reply: "Yes . . ." Their friendship however, will never be as it was before even though Peter does everything he can to pretend nothing has happened.

This father is difficult to speak or reason with. His values stem from the days when people held the firm belief that children would turn out *right* if you told them they were *wrong*.

When this is done with enough conviction and done often enough, and it is supported with a quick smacking then it will seem like it is actually working. Peter will not touch the computer again instead he will become very sensitive to his father's moods and develop an ability to work out when his father is about to explode. He will carefully hide his crushed self-esteem and his loss of trust. He will keep an emotional distance to his father who will never be able to find out what is really happening.

Children are not harmed by their parents' emotions. When, and if, they are harmed it is because of the words which accompany the feelings. Children know about sadness, anger, rage and frustration. They do not like to be scolded, neither do they like it when their parents argue, but they are not harmed by this. On the contrary, it helps them develop a loving, realistic and appropriate understanding of their own emotions.

In families where parents take pride in always maintaining a reasonable, well-balanced and nice atmosphere the children conclude that they are the ones who are wrong. It is perfectly alright being unreasonable every now and then. Unreasonable emotions, unreasonable limits and unreasonable needs are just fine and they are very human. It is an indication that we are living human beings who have not been reduced to actors whose most important roles are to been seen as nice and accepted by their surroundings.

Criticism is different and children really ought to walk around with big placards saying: **"Sorry, but I can't take criticism!"** Underneath there should be a neat and official seal stating: **"Criticism is a serious health hazard. *The Department of Health"***

When an 18 month old toddler is about to pull the books, vases and everything else off the shelves it is a good idea to stop him by saying: "Stop! I don't want that!" If this does not help then it is also alright to physically remove him.

It is however, not alright saying "No . . . ! Now you are not behaving like my good little boy. You must stop when your mother says so!" An 18 moths old is neither "good" nor "bad" in a situation like this. He is curious and full of vigor to explore the world. When he starts kindergarten and has become too scared to venture out into unknown territory his hard fought restraint will most likely be the cause of some questioning comments.

What about the books and vases on the shelves? They can be saved without breaking—even without breaking his soul.

Our mouth and hands are often faster than our brains. We tend to criticize, belittle and cross their boundaries before we get a chance to think about it. There is nothing to do about that—other than make sure the children understand that it was not their fault but our responsibility.

One of the reasons why we often speak or act before we think is because we deep down would like our children (partners and good friends) to have everything we have. We end up giving them so much—more than we are really prepared to give. When they front up and want more we feel they cross our boundaries: "There has to bee a limit!"

Adults are in control over how much they are willing to receive from others. Children are not! Their total existence—especially the first couple of years—depends and relies on their parents doing what is right. For themselves and for the children.

CONFLICTS: TO BE AVOIDED OR CONFRONTED?

Why do conflicts occur

Conflicts happen when two people want something different. Within a family it rarely happens that two people want the same thing at the same time. This means there are plenty of opportunities for conflicts. On most occasions adults as well as children are able to control their needs and wants and cooperate with each other.

We are only able to cooperate if we are not told that our individual needs and wants are wrong even though they are different from others. When we are told they are wrong we are unable to cooperate let alone wholeheartedly be part of the community. We have to give in and compromise ourselves. This is a waste of time and a waste of life.

Infants express their needs and wants instantly. When they learn to speak they are able to express these more clearly and personally. They have no idea about the fact that their parents also have needs and wants and therefore constantly have to consider everyone's requests. This does not mean the children are anti-social by nature, it just means they are inexperienced.

New parents are constantly confronted by the necessity for them to set aside their own needs out of consideration for the well-being and survival of their children. The experience of *giving* as well as *giving up* parts of our lives has significant impact on us. It is enriching as well as frustrating. Enriching because we receive instant and visible feed-back. The child grows and thrives. The stomach functions well or is troubled. The face smiles or cries. You tuck them in and they sleep. You cough and they wake up.

Within a few months we get so used to this "instant feed-back mechanism" that we tend to forget that we are also making a long-term investment from which we will not reap the rewards for another three, five or twenty years.

Some of this early life is frustrating. No one is able to live a fully satisfying life when they have to sacrifice so much of their own for others. Unless, of course we can convince ourselves that the meaning of life is to be there for others. Even so, the expectation of some kind of reward is hidden just below the surface.

When children are around 12 month old it is to a greater extent possible to create a better and healthier balance between theirs and your needs. At that point in time it become important for the parents to demonstrate their own needs. In words as well as in actions: through dialog and negotiations.

What do we believe in?

When they turn 12 month old it is a good idea to reconsider your values once again. This means things can be balanced and make sense. Otherwise, the one who is best able to draw attention to his/her needs will always come first.

There are basically three family styles to choose from:

1: The patriarchal family

Adults assume that they know what is best for the child in any situation. In that case the parents' needs and priorities will reign supreme.

A generation or two ago this was the only thinkable way of parenting. There were no other options available.

2: The democratic family

Adults assume that the children know their own needs better than anyone else. It is therefore important that the children get what they need and thus the children's wishes and needs become the central and focal point of the family.

This is the opposite of the patriarchal family structure and many modern families believe it to be the only real alternative.

3: The family based on equal dignity

Adults may assume that the family as a living arrangement only makes sense and provides opportunities if every single member's needs are considered equal and that these needs should be met if possible.

This is the family I call: "The family based on equal dignity".

It is obviously only in writing that it is possible to define things so simply. Real life is much more complex and nuanced. This is a particular reality for families who have had children since the late 1980s. They are in the middle of a period of transition where all three family styles blend together in mixed quantities. Essentially, it is irrelevant which of the above families yours is most similar to as long as it suits everyone who is part of your family.

The *patriarchal family* is probably the most widespread family style in most parts of the word. It is almost dominant in areas where women are not yet able to enjoy basic human rights. The patriarchal family style also exists in a *matriarchal* version. When considering the family's long-term health and well-being the patriarchal family is a disaster. Nevertheless, it does provide a degree of calm and stability in terms of power structure and allocation of power. The research which comes out of Scandinavia shows that children who suffer from psychological and social problems often grow up in these patriarchal families.

The *democratic family* adheres to a philosophy which believes in the equal sharing of power. However, after a couple of years they tend to descend in to a rather primitive democracy where neither adults nor children thrive. There are plenty of very successful exemptions and the rules of democracy have indeed been beneficial to those families. I have on a number of occasions [1] described these families as "service families". I do this because the parents become so occupied with servicing their children's wishes and needs that their own fade away.

Part of the problem, which I shall elaborate on later, is that it can be difficult to see the difference between what children *want* and what they *need*. Parents' attempts to service is a genuine expression of their love and their involvement in their children's lives. As we know, children *want* anything and everything all of the time so servicing them becomes all consuming.

The issue is not the *love* but the *service*. Similarly: toys are not love but simply toys, and money is not love either but just money. This is why many children very quickly experience a greater and greater need for love. Out of consideration for their parents' way of showing love they will demand more and more service.

---

[1]   Jesper Juul, Dit kompetente barn, Kbh. 1995, s. 120 ff.

While parents suppress their own needs the less *personal* and the less *present* they become. Love without presence is like a menu without a meal: you become extra hungry.

As a result children can become a nuisance to those around them. They will treat every community as if it exists exclusively for them. This is not because they are anti-social but because this is the way their family operates and the only way they know.

A way out of this vicious circle is *not* for the parents to set limits *for* their children or learn to say "No!" rather than "Yes!" The solution is for the parents to establish (or re-establish) their own needs and wishes and to be courageous enough to express them as well as insist on them being taken seriously. Parents do not need to say "No!" to their children, they need to learn to say "Yes!" to themselves. As soon as that happens the annoying child will disappear and become very pleasant to be around.

It is an interesting paradox of our culture that we consider children with aggressive and self-asserting behavior as "wrong". Whereas those with self-destructive behavior we think of as "innocent". As if either is unhappier or in greater pain than the other.

Princes and princesses

These days more than ever before some parents wait for years before they have their first child. The child soon becomes the "prince" or "princess" of the family. This status then entitles the child to receive the finest clothes, the most expensive and latest toys and will on any occasion be admired and adored.

There is little difference between "service" and admiration or adoration: it is meant well but it does not involve any closeness or connection with the child. After a few years the child will start behaving just like a real prince or princess and rule the family.

Parents become confused and frustrated: "We have given her *everything* and look how ungrateful she is!" Then they give her presents less frequently and the princess is punished until she finally breaks down and becomes very humble and perhaps even subservient. Her crime was simple naiveté: she did not realize that even though the presents had "love" written all over them, they might not contain any warmth at all.

When you are the center of attention you are not, and cannot be, part of that community.

As times passes she will learn to avoid making her parents angry but she will never heal on the inside. She will always remember her "wonderful" time as a princess. It is also most likely that she will repeat her parents' mistake when she has children of her own.

Healthy conflicts

Families who endeavor to create more equal relationships will inevitably experience regular conflicts between the adults' and the children's needs. It is therefore helpful to understand the healthy and natural elements of a conflict. This is especially helpful if we consider tears and frustrations as something negative—just like Caroline's parents did in the previously mentioned "ice cream" example.

All of us are born with the ability to live through conflicts in ways that enable us to deal with them constructively and grow from these experiences. For a number of reasons many parents have forgotten this skill or been led to believe that it is "childish". They have stopped doing it and encourage their children to "grow out of it". This is a pity as it is the only way we are able to stay mentally healthy throughout our lives. There is no room for this ability in public or at work which makes it even more important to create room for it within the family.

Caroline is a completely healthy child. When she wants ice cream she opens her mouth and makes it known. If she cannot get it easily then she will try to get it by other means. If that fails she cries (mourns). This takes a little while and then she calms down. After this journey her parents can feel proud and celebrate that their child continues to be healthy. There is nothing to worry about and absolutely no reason to feel guilty.

Many parents recognize this pattern from their older children who desperately try to make their parents give them what they want. When they realize they cannot get it they storm into their room, slam the door and throw themselves on the bed and bury their teary head in the pillow. If you enter their room straight away to comfort or talk to them you will most likely be yelled at. What they are really saying is: "Please don't interrupt my process of mourning, otherwise I'll not be able to get over my frustration!" Try to cope and wait. Perhaps you can carefully put your hand on their shoulder and you might be allowed to stay.

As they grow older children will develop a greater sense of proportion. They will no longer burst out crying straight away. They will become a little sad and quiet. Parents often misinterpret this as "sulking" or being "grumpy". This misunderstanding also often happens between adults. It is very important to be able to and allowed to mourn when you have lost something—whether this is a good friend, a family member, a pet or the anticipation of an ice cream. Adults as well as children can do this on their own but it is better to be able to do it with someone who understands that an ice cream is the most important thing in the whole world when you are 18 month old.

If we are able to keep this skill alive the quality of our relationships with other people will reach different dimensions. We learn to take responsibility for our own lives instead of blaming others for our misfortunes. Caroline is in the middle of her first lesson: you cannot always get what you want and the only thing you can do is have a good old cry about it. She is not *being unreasonable* neither is she *making a fuss*. She does not have to *come to her senses* or be a *big girl*. She is exactly the way she ought to be. While she is crying about the ice cream she is missing out on, her parents need to enjoy the wonderful child they do have.

Sad or just frustrated?

It is a good idea to work out when your child is sad or just frustrated. Especially in relation to conflicts. In small children the difference is difficult to notice but it is possible if you listen carefully. Frustration is a necessary part of any learning process and childhood is a very long one. It is not until we grow into adulthood that we learn to deal with some of our minor frustrations in silence. Essentially, there is no difference between a two-year-old throwing her spoon on the floor because the food slipped off and a fully grown man angrily kicking a flat tire.

When children are frustrated they do not need to be comforted as if they were sad. They might need some help handling the spoon, the LEGO car or the maths challenge. When they are frustrated with their parents they either need to be left alone or simply have their frustration acknowledged in a way which makes them understand that it is alright. Previous generations would say: "Sulking doesn't help!" Parents thought the children were sulking as a way of manipulating. They did not understand that it was a way for the children to regain their inner balance.

Children become sad when they lose something which matters to them: a pet, a friendship, their parents understanding and love, confidence in their parents—and when their parents separate. Then they need all the closeness, understanding, empathy and patience you can possibly mobilize.

Children are obviously different and have each their own way of telling their parents when they have experienced an appropriate amount of closeness and when they feel smothered. The latter often happens when we cannot handle their sadness and try to repress it before they have finished living through it.

Confrontation and closeness

A confrontation is not necessarily always heated and emotional. A confrontation simply means that one person wants something and another something else—and that both of them are prepared to speak their minds.

The parent says: "You'll have to brush your teeth before you go to bed!"

The child replies: "I don't want to!"

When a confrontation occurs it is not a good idea to try to *divert* the issue. In the above situation many parents would say: "I have found a really good story we can read when you have brushed your teeth and are in bed!" It might make the child brush his teeth that particular evening but the long-term consequence is that you teach the child how to *manipulate*.

In a situation like that when there is no room for negotiation it is much better to give the child a bit of time. Wait five minutes, nudge him and say: "Are you ready to brush your teeth?"

This little bit of *time* is an often overlooked "wonder drug" in relation to conflicts with children of all ages. It is a good idea to give the child five minutes, two hours or a few days depending on the type of conflict. The reason for this lies deep inside the core of being a child.

Exactly like adults, children need time when they have to do something they do not really want to do. They need time to move into a position where they are able to say "Yes!" Are they not given that time all they can do is say "Yes Sir!" and let go of their personal dignity. They may well *chose* to accept this kind of obedience on the sports field or at kindergarten but in relation to their parents they do not have a choice other than to hand over their personal dignity.

Children are so focused on *cooperating* with their parents that they see it as suspicious and insulting when they force them to cooperate. In the child's perception of the world the above example is not a question about brushing teeth. He feels that his love for his parents is being questioned because they do not seem to trust him. Understanding this reality makes it easier to prioritize what is important.

When parents give their children just a little bit of *time* many pointless and draining conflicts can be avoided. However, if *time* is used as a trick for parents to get thing their way it does not work. As usual, children are just like adults. We enjoy cooperating when at all possible but do not like to be manipulated into doing it.

Conversation and negotiation

When the wishes and needs of children and adults are at odds dialog and negotiation is required. It is important to remember that it is the quality of the *process* and not of the *content* which is most important for the well-being of the family. This quality often requires careful consideration. It might also require plenty of time. However, a *personal* conversation is substantially shorter than an *impersonal* conversation. The quality of the conversation is more important to the family's well-being than the outcome.

There is no such thing as an easy-to-follow method or a set structure for this kind of conversation. There are some broad guidelines and principles (as presented in this book) which you might want to consider or even try. But beware, there is no "method".

This obvious lack of method is unique to human relations as they are built on our love for each other. We might be able to learn how to relate to colleagues at work, to our superiors, to the neighbor, and so forth. This is all about learning certain rituals. We are also able to learn how to train dogs and break horses as it requires certain techniques. This is not the case in relation to those we love. Methods and techniques erase our individualities and with that our equality.

Every single day we are forced to face the uncertainty of experimenting our way through life. What worked for us yesterday might not work today simply because we constantly develop on a personal level. This is different to most other interactions we have, as these require us to perform certain roles which are reasonably consistent. When they change we can easily modify and learn the new rules that apply. Within the family our challenge is different, namely to take others' wishes and needs seriously, as seriously as we consider our own—or take our own wishes and needs as seriously as we take others'—depending on your starting point. Adults and children have something very interesting in common: when we feel that our wishes and needs are taken seriously it becomes less important to be right and get things our way.

An example:

When Christian asks: "Can I stay at Frederic's tomorrow night?" His father answers: "No Christian. You are not allowed to do that. Occasionally we would like to spend some time with you as well!" Then two different wishes are opposing.

Had Christian's father said: "I'm not sure. Is something important happening?" then he is inviting his son to elaborate further. This is a good thing for Christian who feels he is taken seriously. It is also a good thing for his father who is able to work out what he really needs to consider—apart from which bed Christian should be sleeping in the following night.

If Christian straight away had told his father why he wanted to stay over at Frederic's then he would have been arguing for the *cause*. With the father's invitation Christian experiences an interest in his *person*. Consequently, the father does not need to come up with a series of counter arguments. Instead he can focus on *who* he is. He might say: "I am going to be away quiet a bit next week and I really want to spend some time with you this week."

Perhaps Christian decides to spend time with Frederic. Perhaps the father decides to exercise his power: "I understand that you prefer to stay over at Frederic's but I want you to stay home." It is much easier for Christian that someone decides over him when he is being taken seriously.

An evening in the company of *this* father might actually be something he can look forward to. He just needs 30 minutes or so to "say goodbye!" to his plans to stay at Frederic's.

Invitation to conversation

There are in fact many parents who find it difficult taking *themselves* seriously. This is because very few people took them seriously when they grew up. This obviously makes it difficult taking your own children seriously. Nevertheless, it is possible if you have an adult partner to work with. Some support and help is important otherwise the children might take over or the never ending power struggles will drain you completely.

An important aspect of the *quality* of the interaction is that the parents show some initiative and invite the children to elaborate on their wishes and needs. Otherwise children will not learn how to talk about themselves. Instead they will only learn how to argue. If that happens everyone will grow further and further apart and eventually reach the conclusion that there is no point in using words when in conflict with other people.

Expressions such as those below are examples of how parents are able to encourage informative and constructive negotiations.

—I am not sure I understand . . . Tell me a bit more . . .

—I would like to hear why this is important for you . . .

—I find it difficult to imagine that someone would . . . so I am curious, what would make you . . .

—I am not sure what to say to that. You must help me. Tell me why you would like to . . .

These conversations can form the basis for well-considered decision making which respects the dignity and boundaries of everyone.

Small children, especially before they start school, will constantly *cooperate* with their parents. This might not be imminently evident by the way they behave. However, "behind the scenes" they are working very hard on learning from their parents how to be human beings and how to interact with other people. The *way* we conduct ourselves when we are in conflict with them will be thrown straight back at us later on. The better we are able to take them seriously the more seriously they will take us.

Children will pick one parent as their primary and most influential role model. Most families are aware of this but express it differently: "This boy is his father through and through!"

Children relate and connect with one of their parents in particular. This is not an emotional choice. It is not because the child loves one parent more than they do the other, neither is it because one parent loves the child more than the other one does. Science has not yet been able to establish why this connection is established. What we do know is that it has serious consequences if that parent for whatever reason ceases to part of the child's daily life. The parent who is left alone certainly faces serious challenges as well. It is not possible for this parent to give the child what he or she misses regardless of how lovingly and responsibly they try.

It is from one parent in particular that the child learns how to handle conflicts. Internal conflicts as well as conflicts with others. This is important because more often than not it is the one who is most similar to the child who experiences the conflicts as confronting. It is not always enjoyable to look at yourself in the mirror. It does however, highlight how important it is for the parents to *accept responsibility* for conflicts instead of passing the blame to the children.

Children take their parents wishes and needs seriously to the same extent as parents take their children's seriously. The initiative lies with the parents—it all begins with them.

The following applies to any relationship between adults and children. (It is particularly important to remember if you live in a "patchwork family" or "bonus family"—a mixed family or step family.) Bonus parents must try to be as authentic and personal as humanly possible in relation to their new partner's children. Or more to the point: you will be rejected very quickly and decisively if you are not.

All upbringing is to an extend a violation of the children's boundaries. No matter how just or fair you are, upbringing is also manipulation. When we treat children properly they gladly accept being brought up by their biological parents. They do this because they love their parents unconditionally and do not doubt their love.

Children are certainly able to accept a new adult in their life. It may take time because the child will not accept the new parent until he or see feels that this new adult is good for their biological mother or father. However, the children will not tolerate being brought up by them until they are certain that this new adult knows and respects them exactly the way they are. This is the only substitute for unconditional love which children will accept. It might take five or six years before the adult finally qualifies.

Many bonus parents (step parents) have had very painful experiences because they were not aware of this. They entered the new family fully engaged and ready to take full responsibility only to experience constantly being rejected: "You are not my *real* father!"

They did not realize that this really means: "I am not willing to let you fully enter my life until you have qualified. I need to make sure I trust you enough before I'll let you have any influence on the way I develop. I don't want you to go away—you just need to take a few steps back."

Bonus parents must try to befriend their partner's children before they can take part in their upbringing. This challenge is not handed to biological parents until they have finished raising the children.

"NO!"—a most loving answer

For generations parents have said: "Children must learn to understand that "No!" in fact means "No!"" The time has now come for parents to learn this as well.

I believe that most of us are somewhat romantic at heart. We feel most successful when there is a harmonious atmosphere in the family. We simply prefer "Yes!" to "No!" This is partly because of the demands and expectation which reigned in the traditional patriarchal family. "Yes!" is seen as loving and as a sign of unity. But I think there is more to it.

Any loving relationship begins with a "Yes!" A "Yes!" to each other as partners and most of the time an unconditional "Yes!" to the children when they arrive. Saying "Yes!" as often as possible is very much what love is all about—even if we are not always able to wholeheartedly support it. We are not only in love with each other but also with the consistency, the agreement, the solidarity, the unity and the connectedness.

Usually five to ten years pass before we really start noticing the imbalance. The issue is not that we have said "Yes!" to each other or to the partnership too many times, but that we have not said "Yes!" to ourselves often enough.

The children will notice this imbalance very quickly. This happens after two or three years when they begin to say "No!" to their parents and thereby "Yes!" to themselves. They break free of our total care and start wanting to do things on their own: "I want to!" At the same time their individuality becomes more apparent and we notice greater differences between them and us. This comes with their ability to speak and express themselves.

When the children say "No!" it is in fact a loving answer. It is not a "No!" to the relationship with their parents. It is their way of saying "Yes!" to themselves and their way of *defining* themselves as separate from their parents. Children who are two years old are only able to think in small snippets and express themselves in abstracts. This is why they say "Yes!" to themselves by saying "No!" to something tangible, such as putting their shoes on, brushing their teeth, dressing, walking the streets without holding hands, and so forth.

In spite of this children do prefer to cooperate and say "Yes!" to their parents—but only if their "No!" is being respected. To do this means that you need to acknowledge it and take it seriously. You do not necessarily have to do as they say.

This is very similar to the way parents interact with each other. We prefer to say "Yes!" and tend to say it too often and often to the wrong things. Some do this because they see it as their duty or responsibility others because they are worried about the consequences if they say "No!" Some because they are insecure and some even do it because they love the other so much that they have forgotten about themselves.

For many of us it is in fact so important to say "Yes!" and so difficult to say "No!" that we almost sound aggressive when we finally say "No!" or we end up spending hours justifying ourselves. It really is difficult saying "No!" to others with a clear conscience and feeling okay about doing it.

The problem about saying "Yes!" is that we end up expecting others to say the same to us. If this tendency is allowed to develop it easily ends up becoming some kind of complicated calculation with individual scores and totals. ("I always say "Yes!" to you—even when I don't necessarily want to. I think you owe me . . . !") Family life becomes a duty rather than a gift. Within a few years we might end up with "loyalty awards" where the rewards can never be redeemed. Instead we end up paying penalties.

This makes it important for the family's well-being that we learn to say "No!" to each other and feel okay about it—and support each other on that journey.

—You said "Yes!" but it seems like you really meant "No!"

—It is alright for you to say "No!" if that is what you really mean.

Most of us have been taught to do the opposite: when we anticipate that another person will say "No!" we quickly start to persuade and convince them. This might work right here and right now but in the long run you will be paying dearly with more conflicts and a greater personal distance.

The reason for this is very simple and something which all people of all ages have in common: only when we feel free to say "No!" and our "No!" is being respected will we also fee liberated enough to say "Yes!" to each other with all of our heart and soul. Otherwise we are only able to utter a half-baked "Yes!" which very soon will become a big and loud "No!"

In those families where it has become acceptable to say "No!" it turns out that after a while they stop saying "No!" as often as they used to.

The "No!" we are talking about is not a rejection of the community but a "Yes!" to ourselves *within* that community. The benefit is that every member of the family learns to take responsibility for themselves. People who are able to take that responsibility tend to take greater responsibility for other as well.

This is not a question about everyone doing whatever they *desire*. The principle of *desire* is not one which we can base our lives on. This is only a childhood fantasy (and that of a consumer society). It is all about feeling liberated enough to express your individuality. By doing that it becomes possible for the other family members to work out how yours can be included and how to create enough space so everyone fits in.

It will always be the parents who lead and decide although they must let go of some of their traditional power. They need to make up their minds. Either "Do as you are told! Now—or else . . . !" has to go completely or it has to stay. This depends on what kind of family you want.

The right to say "No!" and "No more!" to the children is also about the parents' right to set boundaries for themselves. It is a way they can define themselves in relation to the children. When a "No!" to their children is also a "Yes!" to the parents own important and personal needs then it is a loving "No!" If it is said in self-defense it has already gone too far. Parents turn themselves into victims and their children become the culprits.

This applies both ways. If parents want their children to respect their "No!" then they must show respect for the children's "No!" as well.

On occasions the children's "No!" is of importance to their lives and must be dealt with. Most of the time the "No!" has no real impact and then it is often a question of *time* before the "No!" automatically turns into a "Yes!"

—Would you please hang the washing out?
—No, I don't like doing that.

—That's fine. You don't have to like doing it. It is alright to dislike it—as long as you do it.

—Arhh! You are so annoying! I am watching a movie right now!

—I can see that but I would like you to do it anyway.

Many modern parents feel guilty. They often say "Yes!" to themselves by investing a substantial amount of time and energy in their own careers, at work or on their education. They do this for a variety of reasons and it is tempting for them to make up for this by letting go of their personal boundaries when they finally spend time with their children. They start servicing them and doing things for them more often than is good for anyone involved.

The mathematics of love do not add up like that. A "Yes!" in one area cannot be compensated for by a "No!" in another. This does not work between adults either. The less time parents spend together and the less time they spend with their children the more important is it to be authentic when they are together. The obvious risk is that the children become unhappy with their parents but that is ultimately much better for everyone than if they become unhappy with themselves.

Every member of the family has a desire to say "Yes!" to cooperation and feel as valuable partners in each other's lives. Not until we are able to incorporate "No!" into the family can we avoid that this desire becomes a duty, or that love turns into guilt.

Wants and needs

There is one very important reason why parents ought to define their personal boundaries, set limits for their children and use their power: children do not know what they need. They only know what they want.

That is not exactly correct. Children do *know* what they need they are just not able to use language to express this. They are rarely able to express their fundamental needs but they are able to let the world know when these are not being met.

As they are not yet able to express their needs verbally, they change their behavior instead. They cannot say: "Listen, I really need to be *seen* and *acknowledge* as who I am!" Instead they withdraw or make sure to draw attention to themselves. This will happen at home if they sense that there is still a chance that their parents will respond in a positive and constructive manner. However, more often than not it will happen in kindergarten, at school or in the streets.

It is clearly our responsibility to listen carefully to what our children want and do not want. You do not need a psychology degree to work this out when she wants an ice cream or a doll. That is straight forward. It is when she starts pestering and creating conflicts that she needs neither an ice cream nor a doll. She needs something entirely different and you have to find out what that is.

Children's *wants* should not rule the family. If they get everything they want they will certainly not be getting what they really need: close and intimate contact with responsible adults.

It is obviously a good idea to ask the children: "What do you want for dinner?" It is however, not a good idea if you feel you have an obligation to give them what they want just because you asked. When you prepare dinner you must consider three simple questions: What would the children like? What would the adults like? and How can you serve healthy and varied meals? The latter is obviously your responsibility. You also need to consider how to balance enjoyment, aesthetics and the quality of the food, and make sure you do not implement some strict and dogmatic rules about how often you have pizza in front of the television.

This applies to all other issues as well. It is important that every family member feels free and is able to express what they want. This should be the *beginning* of a conversation not the *end* of one.

Children will be lonely, sad and miserable when their *wants* rule the family. This is not a question about whether or not you are spoiling the children. It does not make sense to ration their "wish allowance" so they only get what they want every second time they ask. Spoiling children does not mean that they get too much of what they *want.* It means they get too little of what they *need.*

Rules and structures

Many parents try to prevent conflicts by implementing a number of rules. This is not an unusual method in our society where laws and regulations are introduced when we are not able to solve things through dialog.

Within the family there are broadly speaking two types of rules. Practical house rules: You wipe your shoes on the mat, put your dirty plates in the kitchen, let your family know if you arrive home late, and so forth. These rules make sense and are good for the family's well-being.

The other types of rules are those parents make up when they do not know how to deal with a conflict: If you don't behave properly you are not allowed to play with Peter. If you don't eat your dinner you cannot have dessert. When I ask you to do something, you do it without discussion. Speak properly to each other. And so forth.

The rule of thumb is that the more of these rule you have the worse your family thrives. The same applies in kindergarten, at school and everywhere else where people need to be together. The trouble with these rules is that they are absolutely *impersonal* and at the same time challenge something deeply *personal*. This duality forces children to invent ways of disobeying the rules in an effort to protect their individuality and dignity without being criminalized.

The need for the practical house rules vary greatly from family to family and from culture to culture. The larger the family the more rules are needed and the more important is it that everyone does their utmost to follow them. They serve some impersonal and practical purposes and are by nature easier to follow.

Many families with children live very structured lives. This is necessary for logistical reasons.

We can make children cooperate with just about anything but there is a price to pay if they are forced to subject to their parent's need for structure. From time to time it is likely that they will try to "sabotage" the rules and limits they otherwise happily cooperate with.

They might refuse to go to kindergarten for a few days or suddenly hate the babysitter. This is most likely their way of saying that they need to spend a few days alone with their parents where they do absolutely "nothing". It is not until you do "nothing" that you are able to hear your heart beat—and speak.

Adults can to a degree postpone this for a while but children are smarter than that. They know that *now* means "*Now!*" Living cannot be prevented by implementing rules—neither can it be put off until later.

Consequences and punishment

Not long ago parents were convinced there had to be *consequences* if children broke the rules or violated their boundaries. These days more and more parents are turning away from that point of view. This is a good thing.

A "consequence" is really just a nicer word for *punishment*. Sure, the methods of punishment have gradually changed and been up-dated but they have not become more humane or civilized.

Throughout history the leading argument in favor of "consequences" has been the need for children to learn to respect the limits adults set. It is questionable if this aim has ever been achieved. What is certain is the fact that many children have been scared of the consequences. This is a different issue entirely.

It *is* important that children respect their parents and their boundaries. The problem is that by adding the threat of a consequence you say: "I give up making you take *me* seriously. Now I have to replace *me* with a consequence and hope you will have greater respect for that than you have for me."

If this is not a direct admission of failure then it is not far off. The fact is that the adults regularly have to come up with new and increasingly extreme consequences to be able to counteract the children's increasing lack of respect. This will inevitably become a vicious circle or the consequences will become so extreme that the relationship between adult and child suffers irreparable damage.

The alternative requires thee things: patience, repetition and a preparedness to take yourself and the child seriously.

It takes a long time for children to get to know their parent's boundaries so well that they avoid crossing them too often. It is so much easier when the boundaries are clear and personal but even then it takes a long time. Parents need to be aware of this and be patient. Not patient in the sense that the boundaries are introduced bit by bit but patient with the necessary learning process children have to go through if *their* boundaries are not to be seriously violated. Children are not particularly "slow". In fact, it does not take them any longer than it takes two parents to learn each other's boundaries.

Learning to avoid crossing other people's boundaries is not some kind of process which happens automatically—unlike learning not to cross at a red light. You must know and remember the other person's boundaries and at the same time work out how to stay true to your own boundaries in relation to those. We need to say "Yes!" to other people's boundaries without saying "No!" to our own—unless you can accept being reduced to saying "Yes Sir!" Some people even have boundaries which are completely unacceptable to others. It will take even longer to get used to living with them. Perhaps this is why no one is easy to live with . . . ?

When all of this is taken into consideration it is still highly likely that you from time to time violate each other's boundaries. Then parents need to confront their children's dissatisfaction. There is no point in talking about it in the heat of things. "Strike while the iron is cold."

—Listen Nick! For some reason or other you continue to mess up my stuff. I have had enough! I don't want this to continue. I'm not sure why you continue doing it. Do you just forget or do you think it is unreasonable that you are not allowed?

—Dunno! . . . why am I not allowed to?

—I don't want this because they are my things and I want them left alone. I get furious when you forget and I want you to remember no matter whether you think it is stupid or unreasonable. I want my things left alone—end of story!

No promises, no threats and no deals! Any of those would have lessened the confrontation and diverted the attention away from the words and feelings that matter *right now*. Be brief. It is a question about making an impact not about lecturing, convincing or agreeing.

The father in this example makes the biggest impression when he is able to speak about himself as a *person*—the person he feels lacks respect. The more he speaks from his *role* as the parent the less impact he will have. In this instance it is the greatest difference between taking yourself seriously and being pompous.

If the father takes himself seriously and really believes in what he says, then his son will be shaken. He will be sad or angry and perhaps both. This is just fine. It is the way it has to be. If the issue is important it has to be serious.

Many adults want to be nice so they use "child-friendly" language when they speak with children. This *might* be a good idea when it is about something factual the child needs to learn. It is not a good idea in a *personal conversation* like the above. The adult must use adult language—this is *his* language. When adults speak like teachers important nuances of the message will get lost and the conversation will have less impact.

One of the things children need to learn is to take other people and their boundaries seriously. Respect other people simply because they are people. It is not about learning to be afraid of consequences and power. They will only learn to abuse it when they grow older.

The above confrontation is not just about the father making sure he is able to keep his things untouched. It is just as much about teaching the son how to deal with things in the school yard, at work, as a partner and as a father. How he can keep his dignity without violating other's dignity.

Many parents have failed to teach their children this because they were not able to demonstrate it themselves. They have greater faith in consequences than they have in themselves and their children.

Guilt and responsibility

We have children because we want to—it is not because the children want to. The starting point is therefore very self-centered. This is a good thing: we want to enrich our lives and do everything possible to enrich their lives too. Parenthood is all about giving and feeling valued by another person.

This fundamental self-centeredness is balanced out by our preoccupation when the children gradually show us their needs and their personality. Irrespective of the parents' decision to base the relationship on power or equality there is only one goal: giving the child what they believe is a good life.

Parents always succeed—to some extent. There is however, no such thing as a perfect parent. Fortunately, parenting works out just fine for most of us. Children grow up with the parents they happen to have. They have to accept and live with that, just like the parents had to live with their parents the way they were.

The most important quality for children, for parents and for their mutual relationship is the parents' willingness to take responsibility for whatever fails along the way.

All parents stuff up. We have good days and bad days, we are unreasonable and get carried away, we have lots of energy and none at all, we know what we ought to do but do the opposite anyway. We all have good and bad memories of our own upbringings. This enriches our relationships—and puts a strain on them.

Do we need to feel guilty about being human?

The answer is not as easy as the question. When we live with other people we are co-*responsible* for their lives and well-being. When we do something which is destructive to them then we also have to take co-*responsibility* for that.

We can deal with this in two ways: either we feel guilty or we feel liable.

Our ability to feel guilt is one of our human characteristics which distinguishes us from other mammals. This is an important part of being human. Without this, morals and ethics would not exist and we would live by the laws of the jungle.

Feelings of guilt make us react in two ways: Some people become depressed, ashamed and do not have enough energy to alter their behavior in a more positive direction. Others become aggressive and try to pass some of the blame onto others. It is often possible to shift this blame—especially onto a child—yet we cannot get rid of guilt. Consciously or subconsciously it is stored and builds up. It is very likely that this leads to further destructive behavior.

Being consciously aware of our responsibilities and our sense of guilt is just as important as our responsibility to care for our children, playing with them, enjoying them and having fun with them. We need to be aware that even though we try our very best there is a risk we might harm them. This does not mean we need be serious and cautious all the time. We just need to remember to take responsibility for our mistakes.

The best way of doing this is by sitting down with the child and saying: "I did such and such yesterday (or two years ago). That was my mistake—not yours!" When the message is formulates as clearly as that three important things happen:

>—The adult's *acknowledgment* becomes a constructive part of his or her life. Feeling guilty then becomes a precursor to acknowledgment.
>—The child is absolved from his or her feeling of guilt and will simultaneously learn more about how to be a responsible human being [2].
>—The acknowledgment by the adult makes it possible for him or her to behave more constructively in the future. A feeling of guilt tends to exasperate the destructive.

One decisive condition is that the adult does not become sentimental and does not appeal to the child and ask for forgiveness. If so, it becomes the child's responsibility to look after the adult's feeling of guilt. This doubles the child's already heavy burden.

The guilt which many of today's parents feel is not at all clear. It is not a relevant feeling of having done something

---

[2] Jesper Juul, Dit kompetente barn, Kbh. 1995, s. 120 ff.

85

wrong, neither is it simply a guilty conscience. It comes from a general impression that we really ought to be different from the way we are. We ought to have had greater control over our lives and had more time for the children when they were young. We should have prevented the divorce. We should have worked less. Should have, should have, should have . . . !

This general feeling of guilt is absolutely superficial. It does not make you any better or any wiser. It certainly does not benefit your children. Get rid of it and replace it with the only known anti-venom: humor and self-irony.

However, the awareness and the experience of guilt is part of every single family. It goes hand in hand with love. There has to be room for some feelings of guilt within the family—it should just never be allowed to take over.

Children's abilities to cooperate and deal with the conditions of their upbringing will almost never wear out. They will not give up—not even when they are unable to get through to us and tell us that the price they are paying is getting too high.

Their love for us as parents is equally long-lasting. It is the love for themselves which is vulnerable.

Their unquestionable loyalty does in fact make them "unreliable" witnesses. We have to trust our own feelings. If we feel things are going well then there is no reason to change things—not even if the books or super-nannies encourage us to. Children thrive well with parents who are content and pleased with themselves—without being smug.

The issue of defining our boundaries is important but only one aspect of living with children. It is however, the issue which is most provoking and challenging for us as parents and it is what tells our children more about who we *also* are.

When we stop thinking of boundaries as "limits" and "restrictions" everyone will be able to grow beyond their own boundaries.

DEFENSIVE PARENTING

When we are in a "defensive" mode we are in fact sheltering behind a "fence". We adopt a way of being where we hand over the initiative for many aspects of our lives to others. We no longer act on our own behalf but simply re-act to other people's actions. We become victims of our relationships. This is not an uncommon way for parents to relate to their children. Unfortunately, in this situation everyone suffers.

Not long ago, I experienced the following episode at a restaurant in Milan, Italy. Reality is that it could have occurred in Singapore, London, Sydney, Hong Kong, New York, Tokyo or indeed anywhere else in the world.

I was sharing a meal with a journalist from the newspaper, La Repubblica after a press conference. The journalist was hoping for an in-depth interview about family values.

A few minutes into the interview, a family sat down at the table next to ours. There was a young boy aged around three, his mother, father and grandmother. The scenario happened exactly as I describe it below. It was as if I had arranged it in order to answer the journalist's first question: "What are the most typical mistakes young parents make?" A classic *journalist question* which is, of course, impossible to answer. So, the family came in handy.

The first thing both parents did was to ask the boy where he would like to sit. He chose to sit next to his mother but within seconds he threw a tantrum because he did not really want to sit there. His screeching voice was typical for a child who has become a victim at a very young age. The father made funny faces trying to calm him. Then he pulled out a little present. "Who do you think this is for . . . ?" The boy did not answer but jumped out of his chair and pulled the present out of his father's hand.

He could not get the wrapping off so his whining became unbearable. It sounded like he had been hit very hard. The father offered to help but this was rejected outright.

The present, a little electronic game, was bought in the hope of a peaceful dinner without dramas. The father explained that it needed batteries. The boy would not let him put them in—but complained that the toy did not work. About 20 minutes passed and several times the waiter was sent away, as no one had yet had a chance to look at the menu. Each of the adults tried to calm the boy while the others stared intensely at him.

Finally, the boy sat on his father's lap and tried the game. Before the adults chose their meals, they encouraged the boy to tell them what he wanted for dinner—without luck. Then followed a number of suggestions, which were all rejected. Eventually, the mother convinced the boy that he liked gnocchi with tomato sauce.

When the food arrived the father grabbed his son's fork, picked up a gnocchi and tried to feed him. It was too hot and he spat it out with a scream. This was accompanied by a selection of "good" ideas and plenty of accusations by the two women. The atmosphere was not pleasant, nevertheless the adults managed to retain their insincere, child-friendly faces in a gesture of overwhelming kindness towards their little idol.

The adults started their dinners but their total attention and focus was dedicated to finding out what the boy wanted instead of the gnocchi. He rejected every suggestion until the mother convinced him that he would like pizza. It arrived—but was rejected. The mother and grandmother then tried the oldest trick in the book: they each took a little bite of the pizza and exclaimed excitedly how wonderful and absolutely delicious it was. That made no difference. However, when the boy discovered a little dog belonging to other guests the adults gained a few minutes peace. Well . . . it was not exactly peace because they had to pay full attention to the boy and the dog. Nevertheless, they were able to guzzle down their food and the father drank his wine as if it was mineral water.

Back at the table, the boy announced that he was hungry, but he did not want the pizza. After lengthy negotiations he accepted the grandmother's suggestion of chocolate ice cream.

The father clearly disagreed but remained silent. Instead, he ordered a Grappa for himself.

The ice cream arrived, served with much fanfare by the waiter. This time the mother grabbed the spoon and served the boy his first bite. He spat it out complaining that there were no nuts in the ice cream. The mother ate the ice cream while the father ordered another Grappa and paid for the dinner.

This is one of those episodes that makes the current generation of grandparents talk about how spoilt today's children are. It is also what makes psychologist write moralizing best-sellers about those "little tyrants".

When the family left the restaurant the journalist was gob-smacked. She told me that she had just seen a re-enactment of her own family. She was shocked and we spent the next hour going through the various scenarios and discussing the parents' options. She acknowledged that she and her husband (and their three children) belong to a generation which I call "neo-romantics". They immerse themselves into everything their children do. They turn this into their mission and the children become a "project". They have only one aim: a happy and harmonious family. They have read all the right books—but skipped the chapters about the inevitable and necessary conflicts. Instead, they take every little frustration personally, and ultimately, feel that they have failed as parents. Then they will, just like the Italian family, spend all their energy, creativity and love on trying to avoid conflicts and frustrations.

Failing their duty of care

This is a defensive position which many parents develop while their children are very young. They focus on preventing conflicts and try as quickly as possible to stop those that do occur. The result is obviously the exact opposite of what they aim for as they end up with plenty of disharmony and conflicts. They subscribe to the idea that children need a lot of attention and give them twice as much as they really need. The children do not need all this attention, and consequently, they never get the opportunity to learn that other people also have needs, boundaries and emotions.

This way of interacting with children is often interpreted as indulgence and pampering but the reality is that the parents fail in their duty of care. Their children end up paying the price when they eventually need to interact with real people.

The solution is not to implement strict limits and rules or try to "toughen-up" the children. Parents need to understand that their children need adult leadership. They also need to understand that it is perfectly alright to make room for their own adult emotions, desires and needs. This is so important that poor leadership is in fact better than no leadership at all. The leader of the Italian family was the three-year-old boy—as a result everybody suffered. Implementing change is a complex process which often needs therapy and strong support. The parents need to learn how to channel their love in a way that ensures the family is able to thrive. ("Family time" by Juul & Øien, AuthorHouse describes this in greater detail.)

Now the question begs: what should the Italian parents have done in relation to their "difficult" son? The answer is not straight forward and needs to take into consideration the parents' backgrounds and motivations. Nevertheless, these are my observations and my suggestions for them to move forward:

The three-year-old boy set the agenda and controlled the three adults. This could only happen because they *let* it happen. It really is an intellectual issue, which deals with their thoughts, attitudes, perspectives and understandings of themselves as parents, grandparents and partners. In their minds and in their imaginations they dream of (permanently) happy children and a (permanently) harmonious family. Parents have a great variety of reasons for wanting this. They might come from families with many destructive conflicts and plenty of pain. Their aim is to avoid pain by limiting conflicts. Other parents were suppressed, ignored or simply not "seen". Still others believe in a romantic ideology and think the world is a horrible place. They want to shelter their children in a make-believe fantasy. Finally, many parents believe their children need much more attention than they really do.

All of these parents have one thing in common: they willingly become totally self-effacing. They are not aware of this themselves but the reality is that they no longer have respect for their own personal boundaries, needs and values. They end up role-playing and acting like totally accepting, always smiling and constantly flexible parents who provide never-ending service. Their personality as well as their humanity will be erased. They reduce themselves to some kind of adult Teletubbies.

From day one children interpret their parents behavior as an expression of love—even when it, objectively speaking, and in the child's subjective experience, is unloving. This is the reasons why conflicts occur when children are toddlers. At that age they have to get become accustomed to their parents not being able—or willing—to be available 120% of the time as they had been up until then. Suddenly, the love changes character which naturally frustrates them. It obviously takes time for children to get used to these new ground rules.

The root of the problem is therefore an intellectual one. It is not about being lazy or a desire to spoil children. Many parents are simply focused on giving their children the ultimate childhood, and if they have enough money, gifts and goods will follow. The result is always the same: responsibility for the quality of the relationships within the family will slowly but surely be handed over to the children. The parents will obviously not see themselves as irresponsible exactly because they spend so much time and energy trying to be perfect parents.

Competent parental leadership

Once the Italian parents have acknowledged this and are willing to reclaim their responsibility step by step they can start dealing with the conflicts.

This process should ideally begin by both parents sitting down with their son at a time when there is relative harmony between them. Then they say: "Dear Marko, we have now had the pleasure of being your parents for almost four years and we are really happy about that. We are not so happy about the conflicts we get into. Fortunately, we have worked out why they happen. We had completely forgotten that it is up to us as your father and mother to take responsibility for the atmosphere between the three of us. However, we have handed this responsibility over to you—and we are sorry about that! From today you will no longer have responsibility for all three of us. This means that we will make more decisions than you and we are used to and it doesn't matter if you get angry with us. We actually prefer this instead of you thinking that you are wrong." (It is absolutely fine for the parents to cry during this conversation.)

Why is this conversation important?

It highlights that things are going to change—the atmosphere within the family will change as will a number of practical things. It supports the parents' credibility and self-discipline, and relives their son of the heavy burden of guilt which he has amassed so far. When the family is frustrated and not in harmony the children will take the blame. The only way they are able to let go of this guilt is when they hear and experience that the parents take the responsibility away from them. Marco does behave like a tyrant but in reality he is just a frustrated victim. This is why many children can be bribed with praise and rewards—for a period of time. It eases the guilt but it does not remove it.

After this conversation, follows a long period of time (6-12 months) during which the parents need to practice taking responsibility. They also need to reintroduce themselves to the family with their own personalities, boundaries, needs and irrational peculiarities. Not only does Marco need to be relieved from his responsibilities, he also needs to be able to find out *who* his parents are.

Let us now look at what the Italian parents could have done during the dinner. They will most likely continue to experience similar dinners to the one above as it takes time before everyone gets used to their new roles.

Let us imagine they enter the restaurant again. It is not a good idea to ask Marco where he wants to sit. The adults need to sit where they want to and leave the last chair for him. If he is unhappy about that he will say so and then the adults can consider if they want to swap with him. Marco is only used to saying what he does *not* want. This should be followed by a gentle invitation to let him express what he does want. Should he declare that he wants to sit where his mother sits then they can swap—as long as she wants to and does not do it to avoid a conflict.

Perhaps none of the adults want to swap. Then Marco will become highly frustrated. All they need to do is give him a friendly smile and say: "Sure, it is awful but that is the way it is. Anyone is free to say what they would like but that doesn't mean they get it." After a few episodes like this his tantrums will ease and eventually disappear.

Then Marco declares that he is not hungry. The response from the adults is: "Okay!" Then they need to refocus their attention on the delicious dishes on the menu. Perhaps he is not hungry. He might have forgotten to ask his stomach—three-year-old boys tend to forget doing that. If the aroma from the adults' meals does not stimulate his appetite he is definitely not hungry.

If he does want dinner then he needs a friendly response: "Wonderful Marco . . . I was getting worried that you didn't feel like anything tonight." The fact that he was given the time and the opportunity to realize and acknowledge his hunger means that there will not be any conflicts about what he is going to order. He was given the chance to claim his autonomy and independence, which is the only power children want. They are quite happy for the parents to deal with the rest. Initially, there was not room for him to sit where he wanted, but then there was room made for him within the family.

Most of the children I meet are able to learn new and more constructive behavior much faster than their parents. One reason for this is probably that their needs are simple (although their wants and wishes are far more nuanced). Their need is: competent parental leadership. Parents carry a lifetime full of personal experiences and they need more time to find new ways to interact with their children. It is very unfortunate that many of these parents are told to tighten the grip and implement stricter limits and rules for their children. I strongly recommend parents ignore this advice. The children will be made to feel guilty which will only add insult to the injury. Instead, they need to be given the opportunity to step into character and learn how to define themselves better. This learning process might take two or three years but it is worth the effort. Simply diagnosing them is not the solution, especially because the parents really are the ones who need to change.

These days we experience an increasing amount of parents and educators who have witnessed and indeed experienced episodes like the one above. This has made them revive old child-rearing methods which created obedient children who grew up to become neurotic adults. It is very sad indeed. Hopefully, the fact that children confront and challenge their parents' and teachers' hunger for power will make this revival short-lived. Abuse of power is not a productive alternative to powerlessness.

Printed in Poland
by Amazon Fulfillment
Poland Sp. z o.o., Wrocław

58100960R00066